P9-DFQ-153

Ambulances
to the Rescue
Around the World

Linda Staniford

capstone

© 2016 Heinemann-Raintree
an imprint of Capstone Global Library, LLC
Chicago, Illinois

To contact Capstone Global Library please call 800-747-4992, or visit our web site www.capstonepub.com

All rights reserved. No part of this publication may be reproduced or transmitted in any form or by any means, electronic or mechanical, including photocopying, recording, taping, or any information storage and retrieval system, without permission in writing from the publisher.

Edited by Linda Staniford
Designed by Steve Mead
Picture research by Eric Gohl
Production by Aileen Taylor
Originated by Capstone Global Library Ltd

Library of Congress Cataloging-in-Publication Data
Cataloging-in-publication information is on file with the Library of Congress.
Written by Linda Staniford
ISBN 978-1-4846-2752-5 (hardcover)
ISBN 978-1-4846-2756-3 (paperback)
ISBN 978-1-4846-2760-0 (eBook PDF)

Acknowledgments
The author and publisher are grateful to the following for permission to reproduce copyright material:
Alamy: CulturalEyes - AusGS2, 4, Leila Cutler, 17; AP Photo: State Journal/Craig Schreiner, 16, 22 (top); Ellie Kealey Photography: 15; Getty Images: AFP/Peter Martell, 14, Bergwacht Bayern, 19; iStockphoto: Giambra, 7, Liz Leyden, cover, ollo, 11, sturti, 6, swalls, 8; Newscom: Image Broker/Jochen Tack, 5, Robert Harding/Ken Gillham, 12; Shutterstock: Alexander Tolstykh, back cover (left), 13, 22 (bottom), CandyBox Images, 20, i4lcocl2, back cover (right), 18, michaeljung, 21, My Life Graphic, 10, 22 (middle), Tim Large, 9

Design Elements: Shutterstock

Every effort has been made to contact copyright holders of any material reproduced in this book. Any omissions will be rectified in subsequent printings if notice is given to the publisher.

All the Internet addresses (URLs) given in this book were valid at the time of going to press. However, due to the dynamic nature of the Internet, some addresses may have changed, or sites may have changed or ceased to exist since publication. While the author and publisher regret any inconvenience this may cause readers, no responsibility for any such changes can be accepted by either the author or the publisher.

Printed and bound in the USA.
009716RP

Contents

Some words are shown in bold, **like this**. You can find out what they mean by looking in the glossary.

What Are Ambulances?

Ambulances are **emergency** vehicles that are used all over the world. They help people who need **medical** treatment.

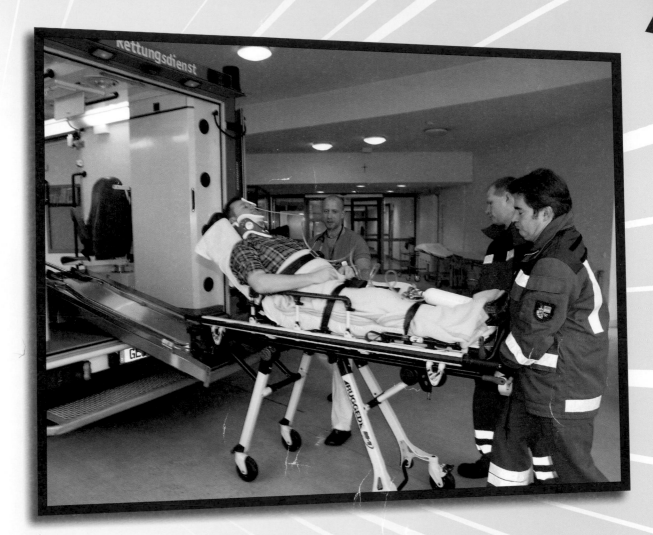

If someone is seriously injured or has an
illness that can't be treated at home,
we call an ambulance. The ambulance
arrives and takes the person to a hospital.

Who Drives Ambulances?

Ambulance crews are called paramedics or emergency **medical** technicians (EMTs). They often wear **uniforms**.

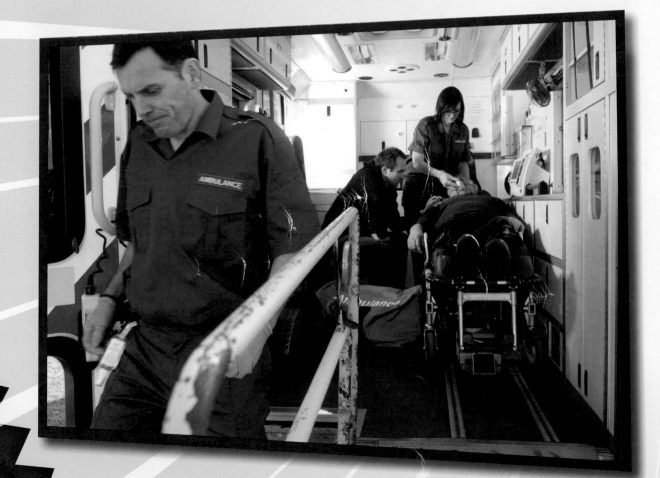

Paramedics and EMTs can deal with all kinds of **medical emergencies**. Often they can treat people without having to take them to the hospital.

What Do Ambulances Look Like?

Ambulances are often painted a bright color such as red, white, or yellow. They have a red or blue flashing light and a **siren**.

Some paramedics and EMTs travel in an **emergency** response car. They can begin to treat the injured person before the ambulance arrives.

What Is Inside an Ambulance?

Ambulances carry lots of different **equipment.** They have stretchers to carry injured people, bandages to treat wounds, and oxygen tanks.

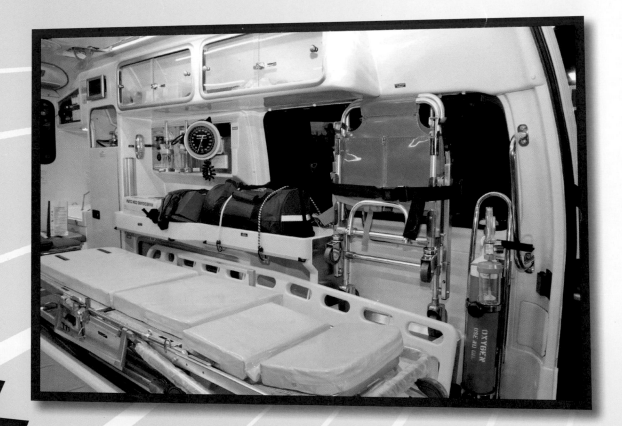

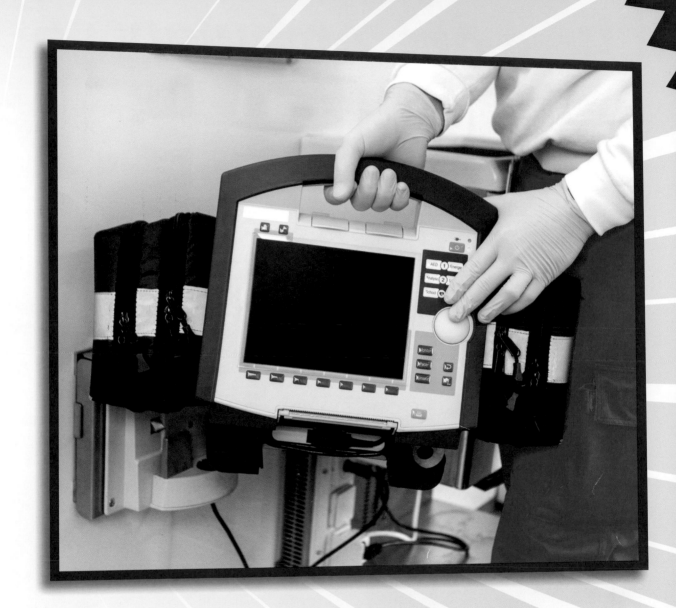

Ambulances also have a **defibrillator**.
This can restart a person's heart if the
heart has stopped beating.

How Are Ambulances Different Around the World?

In Australia, ambulances need to travel over long distances where there are no roads. The Flying Doctor service uses planes and helicopters to reach people who need **medical** help.

In Venice, Italy, people travel on **canals** instead of roads. Boats called water ambulances take people to the hospital.

In South Sudan, Africa, motorcycle ambulances are used to reach people on roads that big ambulances can't reach. They have a **sidecar** for an injured person to ride in.

In Afghanistan, donkey ambulances are used to take people to health centers. The donkeys have a padded seat on their backs to carry the sick person over **rough** ground.

Can Ambulances Travel on Mountains?

Some special ambulances can travel on snow and ice. In Switzerland, these ambulances have runners like skis. They can cross ice to rescue people who are injured while skiing.

In Bulgaria, there are ambulances that run on **tracks** instead of wheels. They can climb up snowy mountains to reach injured climbers.

What If Ambulances Can't Get Through?

Helicopters are used to reach people who are injured on mountains or clifftops where there are no roads. This service is called the Air Ambulance.

People can get injured when they explore caves deep underground. Paramedics and EMTs use special **equipment** to rescue injured people from the caves.

Making the World a Safer Place!

Ambulance workers have a very exciting and **rewarding** job. They help sick and injured people every day. They never know what might happen next.

People who work in ambulances are very brave people. It is good to know we can call them if there is an **emergency**.

Quiz

Question 1
What kind of ambulances can run on snow and ice?
a) helicopters
b) motorcycles
c) ambulances with runners or tracks

Question 2
Which of these are found in an ambulance?
a) stretcher
b) bicycle
c) horse

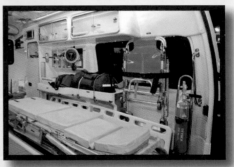

Question 3
What kind of ambulances would you find in Venice?
a) Flying Doctor
b) water ambulances
c) donkey ambulances

Answers: 1c), 2a), 3b)

Glossary

canal human-made waterway

defibrillator piece of medical equipment that applies an electric shock to restart the heart

emergency sudden and dangerous situation that must be handled quickly

equipment machines and tools needed for a job or an activity

medical relating to helping sick or injured people get better

rewarding worthwhile

rough not smooth

sidecar small car attached to one side of a motorcycle

siren device that makes a loud sound

track piece of metal and rubber that stretches around a vehicle's wheels

uniform special clothes that members of a particular group wear

Find Out More

Books

Chancellor, Deborah. *Ambulance Rescue* (Emergency Vehicles). Mankato, Minn.: Smart Apple Media, 2014.

Gregory, Josh. *Ambulance* (Community Connections). Ann Arbor, Mich.: Cherry Lake, 2011.

Internet sites

Facthound offers a safe, fun way to find Internet sites related to this book. All of the sites on Facthound have been researched by our staff.

Here's all you do:

Visit www.facthound.com

Type in this code: 9781484627525

Index